Know Your
Bible
for Kids
Who Is That?

Donna K. Maltese

Illustrated by David Miles

BARBOUR
PUBLISHING

Published by Barbour Publishing, Inc., P.O. Box 719, Uhrichsville, Ohio 44683, www.barbourbooks.com

Our mission is to publish and distribute inspirational products offering exceptional value and biblical encouragement to the masses.

Member of the
Evangelical Christian
Publishers Association

Printed in the United States of America.
United Graphics, Inc., Mattoon, IL 61938-6274; April 2014; D10004436

Introduction

The Bible is a fascinating book. Although it contains hundreds of stories from Genesis to Revelation, it is really one continuous tale revealing not only God's unending love for His people—you and me—but the idea that God has made us unique for a reason! We are each here to play a part in His amazing plan.

Starring in the Bible's many stories are more than 3,000 different people. In this book, we have chosen 99 of the most interesting and important people—both men and women—of scripture. Every sketch follows this outline:

- *Who is this person?*
- *When did he/she live?*
- *What's his/her story?*
- *What's an important verse about him/her?*
- *So what?*

One of the great things about the Bible is the fact that we can learn so much from those who have gone before. We can see ourselves in each story—even though it may have happened thousands of years before we were even born.

Use this fun, fact-filled book to better understand yesterday, guide yourself today, and discover God's plan for your future.

Aaron

Who is Aaron?

Older brother of Moses; Israel's first "high priest"

When did he live?

About 3,500 years ago

What's his story?

One word: Mouth

In more words: God's people, the Israelites, were slaves in Egypt. So God told Moses to go see Egypt's king—or pharaoh—and tell him to free God's people. But Moses had trouble talking. So his brother, Aaron, spoke for him, telling the pharaoh to let God's people go.

Aaron also
- made a golden calf;
- did miracles with his staff;
- wore special robes.

What's an important verse about him?

[The Lord] said, "Is not Aaron the Levite your brother? I know he can speak well. . . . He will be a mouth for you."
EXODUS 4:14, 16 NLV

So what?

When Aaron let others talk him into things that were against God—like making a golden calf for the people to worship instead of God—he got into trouble. But when Aaron listened to God, miracles happened. If you follow God, He'll use you in a mighty way.

Abigail

Who is Abigail?

Widow of Nabal; wife of King David

When did she live?

About 3,000 years ago

What's her story?

One word: Sensible

In more words: Nabal wouldn't feed King David and his men even though they'd guarded Nabal's sheep. So David planned to attack Nabal. But Abigail got some food and rode out to meet David and his army before anyone was harmed.

What's an important verse about her?

[David told Abigail,] "The LORD. . .has sent you today to find me. . . . You have shown a lot of good sense. You have kept me from killing Nabal and his men this very day." 1 SAMUEL 25:32–33

So what?

God is willing to give you good sense to do the right thing in every situation. All you have to do is ask Him.

Abraham

Who is Abraham?

The Father of Many Nations; also called Abram; husband
of Sarah

When did he live?

About 4,000 years ago

What's his story?

One word: Faith

In more words: When Abraham was seventy-five years old, God told him to leave his home in Haran. So Abraham got up and left. He did whatever God told him to do—even sacrificing his own son, who was saved by God at the last minute!

Abraham also

- had two sons, Ishmael and Isaac;
- was very rich;
- believed God's promises.

What's an important verse about him?

Abraham had faith. So he obeyed God. God called him to go to a place he would later receive as his own. So he went. He did it even though he didn't know where he was going.

HEBREWS 11:8

So what?

Like Abraham, you, too, can step out in faith. When you do, good things happen!

Adam

Who is Adam?

The first man; husband of Eve

When did he live?

Day 6 of Creation, thousands of years ago

What's his story?

One word: First

In more words: God created Adam to look just like Him. Then He planted Adam and Eve in the Garden of Eden. God warned them not to eat from a certain tree— but they did anyway. Then they hid from God. But God found them, clothed them, and then kicked them out of Eden.

Adam also
- named all the animals;
- was the father of Abel, Cain, and Seth;
- brought sin into the world by disobeying God.

What's an important verse about him?

And the LORD God made clothing from animal skins for Adam and his wife. GENESIS 3:21 NLT

So what?

Whether you are first or last, good or bad, hiding or seeking, God will take care of you.

Andrew

Who is Andrew?

Fisherman; brother of Simon Peter; disciple of Jesus

When did he live?

About 2,000 years ago

What's his story?

One word: Fisherman

In more words: Andrew was a follower of John the Baptist. When John pointed out Jesus as the Lamb of God, Andrew then followed Jesus. Andrew brought many people to Jesus, including his brother Simon Peter and the boy with five loaves and two fish.

What's an important verse about him?

Peter and his brother Andrew. . .were throwing a net into the lake. They were fishermen. "Come. Follow me," Jesus said. "I will make you fishers of people." MATTHEW 4:18–19

So what?

When you get how great Jesus is, you can't help but follow Him only and bring others to Him.

Anna

A prophet

About 2,000 years ago

One word: Worshipper

In more words: Anna was a very old widow. She worshipped God at the Jewish temple—all day and all night. She even went without food so that she could pray better. When baby Jesus' parents brought Him to the temple, Anna praised God because she knew the child would save God's people.

She talked about the child to everyone who had been waiting expectantly for God to rescue Jerusalem.
LUKE 2:38 NLT

Like Anna, if you spend lots of time with God, worshipping and praying, you will know when His promises come true.

Balaam

Who is Balaam?

A magician

When did he live?

About 3,400 years ago

What's his story?

One word: Untrustworthy

In more words: One day a king convinced Balaam to curse the Israelites. But a talking donkey opened up Balaam's eyes—and ears—to God's will and way. So Balaam ended up blessing, instead of cursing, God's people. Later, Balaam turned away from God again.

What's an important verse about him?

The Ammonites and Moabites had hired Balaam to call a curse down on them. But our God turned the curse into a blessing. NEHEMIAH 13:2

So what?

Don't worry if something not so good happens. God has a way of changing what seems to be bad into something really good. You can trust God!

Barnabas

Who is Barnabas?

An early Christian

When did he live?

About 2,000 years ago

What's his story?

One word: Encourager

In more words: One of the early church leaders was named Joseph. He was such a cheerleader for Christianity, he was nicknamed Barnabas, which means "Son of Encouragement." Because Barnabas had such a good heart, lots of people began following Jesus.

What's an important verse about him?

When [Barnabas] arrived and saw this evidence of God's blessing, he was filled with joy, and he encouraged the believers to stay true to the Lord. ACTS 11:23 NLT

So what?

When we help and cheer on others, we draw them closer and closer to Jesus. Who can you encourage today?

Bartimaeus

Who is Bartimaeus?

A blind beggar

When did he live?

About 2,000 years ago

What's his story?

One word: Determined

In more words: Bartimaeus was a blind beggar sitting by the road in Jericho. When he heard Jesus was near, he began to yell for Jesus to heal him. Others told Bartimaeus to be quiet, but he was too determined. Finally, Jesus called him over and healed him! Then he followed Jesus.

What's an important verse about him?

"Be quiet!" many of the people yelled at him. But [Bartimaeus] only shouted louder, "Son of David, have mercy on me!" MARK 10:48 NLT

So what?

When it comes to faith and prayer, be persistent. Don't let anyone—or anything—stop you from talking to and believing in Jesus!

Bathsheba

Who is Bathsheba?

Widow of Uriah; wife of King David;
mom to King Solomon; ancestor of Jesus

When did she live?

About 3,000 years ago

What's her story?

One word: Coveted

In more words: David wanted Uriah's wife, Bathsheba.
So he slept with her. She got pregnant. So David murdered
her husband and made Bathsheba his queen. But trouble
followed, beginning with the death of their first child.

What's an important verse about her?

David. . .was walking on the roof of the palace. As he
looked out over the city, he noticed a woman of unusual
beauty taking a bath. 2 SAMUEL 11:2 NLT

So what?

God says, "You must not covet" (Deuteronomy 5:21 NLT).
That's because when you want (covet) something that
belongs to someone else, trouble follows. So play it safe—
stay on your own roof and don't take a bath outside.

Boaz

Who is Boaz?

Husband of Ruth; ancestor of King David and Jesus

When did he live?

About 3,200 years ago

What's his story?

One word: Kind

In more words: Boaz was a rich relative of Ruth's dead husband. When Ruth, a foreigner, came to Israel with her mother-in-law, Naomi, Boaz was very kind to Ruth—so kind that he married her! They had a son, Obed.

What's an important verse about him?

[Ruth said to Boaz,] "You have comforted me. You have spoken kindly to me. And I'm not even as important as one of your female servants!" Ruth 2:13

So what?

Boaz's kindness won the hearts of his servants, relatives, and friends. God rewarded him by making him the great-grandfather of a king! Who can you bless with kindness today?

Caiaphas

Who is Caiaphas?

Jewish high priest in Jesus' day

When did he live?

About 2,000 years ago

What's his story?

One word: Know-it-all

In more words: After Jesus raised Lazarus from the dead, Caiaphas worried he would lose his power. So he talked other leaders into having Jesus arrested, tried, and crucified. Little did Caiaphas know that what he did was part of God's master plan.

What's an important about him?

Caiaphas, who was high priest at that time, said, "You don't know what you're talking about! You don't realize that it's better for you that one man should die for the people." JOHN 11:49–50 NLT

So what?

No matter what anyone does—good or evil—God will use it for His own ends. He is the only true know-it-all.

Cornelius

Who is Cornelius?

An Italian army captain from Caesarea

When did he live?

About 2,000 years ago

What's his story?

One word: Giver

In more words: Cornelius prayed to the Jews' God and gave lots of gifts to others. An angel told him to invite Simon Peter to his house. When Peter got there, he preached and the Holy Spirit came. Then Cornelius, his family, and his servants were baptized as Christians.

What's an important verse about him?

Jewish followers who had come along with Peter were surprised and wondered because the gift of the Holy Spirit was also given to the people who were not Jews. ACTS 10:45 NLV

So what?

When you give gifts to God and others, He can't help but give gifts back—to anyone who will take them!

Damaris

Who is Damaris?

A Greek woman

When did she live?

About 2,000 years ago

What's her story?

One word: Convert

In more words: The apostle Paul preached a really good sermon in Athens, Greece, on a rocky hill named after the Roman god of war—Mars. After Paul's speech, Damaris believed in Christ. She converted (or turned) from following many gods to following the one true God.

What's an important verse about her?

Some people followed him and became Christians. One was Dionysius, a leader in the city. A woman named Damaris believed. And there were others also. ACTS 17:34 NLV

So what?

God can use any of us to bring somebody to Christ. Will you let Him use you?

Daniel

Who is Daniel?

Boy brought from Judah to serve foreign kings

When did he live?

About 2,500 years ago

What's his story?

One word: Tamer

In more words: King Darius made a law that everyone had to pray to him. But Daniel would only pray to the one true God, and he did so three times a day. So Daniel was thrown into the lions' den for disobeying Darius. But because Daniel was faithful, God saved him!

Daniel also
- was named Belteshazzar;
- told a king the meaning of his dreams;
- saw the fingers of a human hand write on a wall.

What's an important verse about him?

[Daniel told King Darius,] "My God sent his angel. And his angel shut the mouths of the lions. They haven't hurt me at all. That's because I haven't done anything wrong in God's sight." DANIEL 6:22

So what?

When you make much prayer a habit, God can use you in a mighty way. He may even give you the power to tame beasts!

David

Who is David?

King of Israel; father of King Solomon; ancestor of Jesus

When did he live?

About 3,000 years ago

What's his story?

One word: Praiser

In more words: God chose David to be the second king of Israel. And even though David made lots of mistakes—slept with a married woman, murdered her husband, disobeyed God—he was still the apple of God's eye. Why? Because he gave his full heart to God.

David also
- killed the giant Goliath;
- led a team of 30 mighty men;
- wrote many psalms praising God.

What's an important verse about him?

"God removed Saul and replaced him with David, a man about whom God said, 'I have found David son of Jesse, a man after my own heart. He will do everything I want him to do.'" ACTS 13:22 NLT

So what?

Want to be the apple of God's eye and a giant slayer? Then do everything God asks you to do!

Deborah the Prophetess

Who is Deborah the prophetess?

Prophet and judge of Israel; wife of Lappidoth

When did she live?

About 3,300 years ago

What's her story?

One word: Willing

In more words: The Israelites were being attacked by King Jabin of Canaan. God told Deborah that the Israelites could beat Jabin's 900 iron chariots. But Barak, her army commander, would not lead the men into battle unless Deborah went along. She did, and the Israelites won!

Deborah also
- is the only woman judge of Israel in the Bible;
- usually settled fights while sitting under a palm tree;
- kept the peace in the land for 40 years.

What's an important verse about her?

There were few people left in the villages of Israel—until Deborah arose as a mother for Israel.
JUDGES 5:7 NLT

So what?

When God called on Deborah, she answered, always willing to do whatever He asked. What is God asking you to do? Are you willing?

Delilah

Who is Delilah?

Dangerous Philistine woman

When did she live?

About 3,300 years ago

What's her story?

One word: Greedy

In more words: Samson fell in love with Delilah. Some Philistines, enemies of the Jews, said they would pay her silver coins if she could learn the secret of Samson's strength. She nagged Samson until he finally told her; his strength was in his hair.

What's an important verse about her?

She called in a man to shave off the seven locks of his hair. In this way she began to bring him down, and his strength left him. Judges 16:19 NLT

So what?

Greedy people can be dangerous. Beware of those who love silver and gold more than God and other people.

Dorcas

Who is Dorcas?

Christian from Joppa;
also called Tabitha

When did she live?

About 2,000 years ago

What's her story?

One word: Do-gooder

In more words: Dorcas was a Christian woman who helped lots of people. When she got sick and died, believers sent for Peter. He found Dorcas's body in her room, weeping widows all around her. A few moments later, Peter's faith resulted in a miracle!

What's an important verse about her?

Peter asked them all to leave the room; then he knelt and prayed. Turning to the body he said, "Get up, Tabitha." And she opened her eyes! ACTS 9:40 NLT

So what?

Dorcas used her gifts to do good works in her hometown. What God-given gifts are you using to show the Lord's love?

Elijah

Who is Elijah?

Prophet; miracle worker

When did he live?

About 3,000 years ago

What's his story?

One word: Pray-er

In more words: Because of his closeness to God, Elijah's prayers made miracles happen. They raised people from the dead, made oil appear, brought fire down from heaven, stopped the Jordan River from flowing, and more!

Elijah also

- was fed by ravens, then heard God whisper;
- went up to heaven in a chariot of fire;
- appeared on a mountain with Moses and Jesus in bright light.

What's an important verse about him?

"LORD my God, give this boy's life back to him!" The LORD answered Elijah's prayer. He gave the boy's life back to him. So the boy lived. 1 KINGS 17:21–22

So what?

Elijah did many great and special things. But he was only a human whose real power was in prayer and his special relationship with God. You, too, can be an Elijah! Just keep praying to and listening for God.

Elizabeth

Who is Elizabeth?

Zechariah's wife; John the Baptist's mom; Mary's cousin

When did she live?

About 2,000 years ago

What's her story?

One word: Faithful

In more words: Elizabeth and her husband, Zechariah, were old and had no children. But they stayed faithful to God. One day, the angel Gabriel announced that Elizabeth would become pregnant. She later gave birth to John the Baptist, the one who would call Jesus the Lamb of God.

What's an important verse about her?

The angel said to him, "Do not be afraid, Zechariah. Your prayer has been heard. Your wife Elizabeth will have a child. It will be a boy, and you must name him John."
LUKE 1:13

So what?

God blesses and fulfills the dreams of those who are faithful to Him—during good times and bad.

Enoch

Who is Enoch?

Son of Jared; father of Methuselah

When did he live?

Thousands of years ago

What's his story?

One word: Disappeared

In more words: Enoch was the head of the seventh family that came after Adam. Enoch was 65 years old when his own son Methuselah was born. After that, Enoch walked very closely with God for another 300 years on earth. Then one day, Enoch just disappeared.

What's an important verse about him?

Enoch had faith. So he was taken from this life. He didn't die. He just couldn't be found. God had taken him away. Before God took him, Enoch was praised as one who pleased God.
HEBREWS 11:5

So what?

Amazing things happen when you walk very closely with God.

Esther

Who is Esther?

Orphan girl; King Xerxes' wife and queen

When did she live?

About 2,500 years ago

What's her story?

One word: Risk-taker

In more words: Haman, King Xerxes' top man, decided to rid the kingdom of all Jews. When Queen Esther's cousin Mordecai found out about it, he sent a message to Esther to go before the king to save the Israelites. She did so—even though it might have meant her death.

Esther also

- was a beautiful woman;
- had lots of courage;
- cared more about others than herself.

What's an important verse about her?

"Who knows if perhaps you were made queen for just such a time as this?"
ESTHER 4:14 NLT

So what?

God needs all kinds of people to serve Him at all different times and in all different ways. Ask God how He can use you at such a time as this.

Eve

Who is Eve?

First woman; wife of Adam

When did she live?

Day 6 of Creation, thousands of years ago

What's her story?

One word: Pushover

In more words: God created Eve, a partner for Adam in the Garden of Eden. God told them both not to eat a certain fruit. But a serpent (Satan) easily talked Eve into disobeying God by eating the lovely-looking fruit and offering it to Adam. As a result, sin entered our world.

What's an important verse about her?

The man called his wife's name Eve, because she was the mother of all living.
GENESIS 3:20 NLV

So what?

Eve is the mother of us all. Sometimes, like her, we are easily talked into disobeying God. When you feel tempted, ask God for help. Don't be a pushover for evil.

Ezekiel

Who is Ezekiel?

Prophet and priest

When did he live?

About 2,600 years ago

What's his story?

One word: Messenger

In more words: Ezekiel was given many dreams from God. Visions of flying four-faced angels, battling skeletons, and more contained special messages that Ezekiel was to give God's people. These were dark days when Israel was destroyed and her people taken away from their homes.

What's an important verse about him?

"Son of man, I have chosen you to be a watchman over the people of Israel. Whenever you hear a word from My mouth, tell them of the danger."
EZEKIEL 3:17 NLV

So what?

Even during hard times, God has a good message for believers. Look for it in your Bible.

Ezra

Who is Ezra?

Writer

When did he live?

About 2,500 years ago

What's his story?

One word: Student

In more words: While Ezra was being held captive in Babylon, he studied the Law of Moses. When the king let him go to Jerusalem, Ezra read God's Law to everyone. He also taught the Jews how to apply it to their lives. Because of Ezra, many people turned back to God.

What's an important verse about him?

Ezra had set his heart to learn the Law of the Lord, to live by it, and to teach His Laws in Israel. EZRA 7:10 NLV

So what?

To get a good start in life, be like Ezra—a student of God's Word. Then use what you learn to obey God and help others!

Gideon

Who is Gideon?

Son of Joash; soldier for Israel

When did he live?

About 3,350 years ago

What's his story?

One word: Overcomer

In more words: When called by God to battle his enemy, Gideon thought he was too feeble. But God knew what Gideon was made of—strength, not weakness. The first thing the angel of God said to Gideon was, "Mighty warrior, the LORD is with you" (Judges 6:12).

What's an important verse about him?

Gideon asked, "How can I possibly save Israel? My family group is the weakest in the tribe of Manasseh. And I'm the least important member of my family." JUDGES 6:15

So what?

Believe that God has already given you all the strength you need to serve Him!

Goliath

Who is Goliath?

Giant Philistine warrior

When did he live?

About 3,000 years ago

What's his story?

One word: Darer

In more words: Goliath was huge—more than nine feet tall! And every day on the battlefield, he would dare someone from Israel to fight him. David the shepherd boy took up Goliath's challenge. He shut the giant's mouth, killing him with a sling and one rock!

What's an important verse about him?

David said to Goliath, "You are coming to fight against me with a sword, a spear and a javelin. But I'm coming against you in the name of the LORD who rules over all." 1 SAMUEL 17:45

So what?

Your giant-slaying power is the presence of the Lord with and within you.

Hagar

Who is Hagar?

Slave; mother of Ishmael

When did she live?

About 4,200 years ago

What's her story?

One word: Slave

In more words: Hagar was Sarah's slave. She was given to Abraham so that he could have a son—Ishmael. Later Sarah had a son by Abraham—Isaac. Then Sarah had Abraham send Hagar and Ishmael away. The two almost died from lack of water in the desert.

What's an important verse about her?

God opened Hagar's eyes. And she saw a well of water. She went and filled the leather bag with water and gave the boy a drink. GENESIS 21:19 NLV

So what?

No matter how bad things may seem, God can open your eyes so that you can find whatever you need.

Hannah

Who is Hannah?
Wife of Elkanah; mother of Samuel

When did she live?
About 4,100 years ago

What's her story?
One word: Wholehearted

In more words: Elkanah had two wives—Peninnah, who had children; and Hannah, who did not. Even though Hannah had Elkanah's love, she very much wanted babies. So with all her heart and soul, she cried and prayed to God, who answered her. She gave birth to a baby boy—and then many more!

Hannah also
- named her son Samuel, which means "God hears";
- gave her firstborn son back to God;
- sang a song of thanks to God.

What's an important verse about her?
"I was pouring out my soul to the Lord. . . . For I have been speaking out of much trouble and pain in my spirit."
1 SAMUEL 1:15–16 NLV

So what?
Pray to God with your whole heart. He will hear and answer you again and again.

Herod the Great

Who is Herod the Great?

Part-Jewish, part-Roman king of Judea

When did he live?

About 2,000 years ago

What's his story?

One word: Jealous

In more words: Rome called Herod "King of the Jews." When wise men came to Jerusalem, looking for a just-born king of the Jews, Herod got jealous—so jealous that he had all boys two years old and younger killed. But God had other plans for that just-born king named Jesus.

What's an important verse about him?

An angel of the Lord came to Joseph in a dream. He said, "Get up. Take the young Child and His mother to the country of Egypt. . . . Herod is going to look for the young Child to kill Him." MATTHEW 2:13 NLV

So what?

You can be sure that nothing can stop God and His plans for you—and me!

Isaac

Who is Isaac?

Son of Abraham and Sarah; husband
of Rebekah; father of Jacob and Esau

When did he live?

About 4,100 years ago

What's his story?

One word: Promised

In more words: God promised Abraham that he would
be the father of many nations, beginning with the birth
of a son in Abraham and Sarah's old age. God kept His
promise! When Abraham was 100 and Sarah 90, Isaac was
born—and later saved from being sacrificed.

What's an important verse about him?

The Lord visited Sarah as He had said and did for her as
He had promised. Sarah. . .gave birth to a son.
GENESIS 21:1–2 NLV

So what?

God always keeps His promises. Find them in your Bible
  and claim them all!

Isaiah

Who is Isaiah?

Prophet; preacher; author of the Bible book Isaiah

When did he live?

About 2,800 years ago

What's his story?

One word: Volunteer

In more words: When God wondered whom He could send to speak to His people, Isaiah answered, "Here I am. Send me!" Isaiah later made lots of prophecies about what would happen in the future—and many came true, even those that described Jesus 800 years before He was born!

What's an important verse about him?

Paul said, "The Holy Spirit spoke the truth to your early fathers through the early preacher Isaiah."
ACTS 28:25 NLV

So what?

Like Isaiah and Jesus, you are part of God's plan. When God calls you, will you say, "Here I am. Send me"?

Jacob

Who is Jacob?

Son of Isaac and Rebekah; twin brother of Esau

When did he live?

About 4,000 years ago

What's his story?

One word: Trickster

In more words: Jacob tricked Esau into giving up his rights as the firstborn son. Later, Jacob was often tricked by others. One night, after not letting go of God during a struggle, Jacob was renamed Israel, which means "wrestled with God."

Jacob also
- saw angels going up and down a ladder to heaven;
- got tricked into marrying Leah;
- was father of the twelve tribes of Israel.

What's an important verse about him?

[God told Jacob,] "I am with you, and I will protect you wherever you go. One day I will bring you back to this land. I will not leave you until I have finished giving you everything I have promised you."
GENESIS 28:15 NLT

So what?

Do you have a good hold on God? If so, never let Him go—He just can't wait to bless you.

Jael

Who is Jael?

Wife of Heber the Kenite

When did she live?

About 3,300 years ago

What's her story?

One word: Fearless

In more words: The Israelites' commander, Barak, would not face the Canaanites unless Deborah, an Israelite judge, went with him. So Deborah told him God would hand the enemy's commander, Sisera, over to a woman. That woman was Jael, Heber's wife, who lived in a tent.

What's an important verse about her?

Jael picked up a tent stake and a hammer. She went quietly over to Sisera. . .lying there, fast asleep. He was very tired. She drove the stake through his head right into the ground. So he died. JUDGES 4:21

So what?

God uses ordinary people—like you—to do extraordinary things, all according to His plan.

James, Son of Zebedee

Who is James, son of Zebedee?

Fisherman; brother of John;
disciple of Jesus

When did he live?

About 2,000 years ago

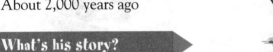

What's his story?

One word: Martyr

In more words: Disciple James, along with his brother
John and their friend Peter, was especially close to Jesus.
All three were with Jesus when He was transfigured and
when He was praying in the garden. James was the first
follower killed (or martyred) for being a Christian.

What's an important verse about him?

King Herod. . .had James killed with a sword.
Acts 12:1–2

So what?

Do you, like James, love Jesus more than life itself?

Jeremiah

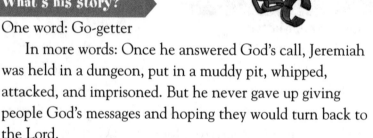

Who is Jeremiah?

Weeping prophet; writer of
the Bible book Jeremiah

When did he live?

About 2,600 years ago

What's his story?

One word: Go-getter

In more words: Once he answered God's call, Jeremiah
was held in a dungeon, put in a muddy pit, whipped,
attacked, and imprisoned. But he never gave up giving
people God's messages and hoping they would turn back to
the Lord.

What's an important verse about him?

"Before I started to put you together in your mother, I
knew you. Before you were born. . . . I chose you to speak
to the nations for Me." JEREMIAH 1:5 NLV

So what?

Imagine—God has known you forever! He knows why you
were made and will help you do what He calls you to do.

Jesus

Who is Jesus?

Son of God; son of Mary; son of foster father, Joseph; the Messiah, the Christ

When did He live?

About 2,000 years ago

What's His story?

One word: Savior

In more words: After the angel Gabriel spoke to a woman named Mary, the Holy Spirit visited her and she got pregnant. She and her husband, Joseph, then traveled to Bethlehem. There, Jesus was born in a stable. Shepherds and wise men bearing gifts came to visit this special child. When He grew up, He told many stories that taught people how to live good lives.

Jesus also
- raised people from the dead;
- cured the sick, lame, deaf, dumb, and blind;
- stopped the wind and waves;
- died on the cross to save us from sin, guilt, and death;
- rose from the dead;
- became the bridge between us and God.

What's an important verse about Him?

In the beginning, the Word was already there. The Word was with God, and the Word was God. . . . All things were made through him. . . . The Word became a human being. He made his home with us.
JOHN 1:1, 3, 14

Then Jesus got up and ordered the winds and the waves to stop. It became completely calm. The disciples were amazed. They asked, "What kind of man is this? Even the winds and the waves obey him!"
MATTHEW 8:26–27

So what?

Jesus, the Word, has been around since the very beginning. He came to earth to save us. When you open up your heart to Him, He lives in you.

When Jesus speaks, amazing things happen. What is He saying to you today? If you're not sure, check out your Bible. What verses really touch you? That's Jesus speaking. Listen, learn, and obey.

Jezebel

Who is Jezebel?

Wife of King Ahab of Israel

When did she live?

About 2,900 years ago

What's her story?

One word: Wicked

In more words: Jezebel worshipped a god called
Baal and a goddess called Asherah. Jezebel wanted the
people of Israel to do the same. She killed a lot of Jewish
prophets. Jezebel talked Ahab into doing many wicked
things, too. And she tried to have Elijah killed.

What's an important verse about her?

"The Lord, the God of Israel, says. . . 'The dogs will eat
Jezebel in the land of Jezreel. No one will bury her.' "
2 KINGS 9:6, 10 NLV

So what?

Wicked ways lead to wicked ends. Stay close to God, do
good, and all will be well.

Joanna

Who is Joanna?

Wife of Cuza

When did she live?

About 2,000 years ago

What's her story?

One word: Provider

In more words: Joanna, who had been healed by Jesus, became one of His followers. Because she was married to Cuza, the man who ran King Herod's household, she had enough money to buy supplies for Jesus and His twelve disciples.

What's an important verse about her?

It was Mary Magdalene, Joanna, Mary the mother of James, and several other women who told the apostles what had happened. LUKE 24:10 NLT

So what?

Joanna saw the angels in Jesus' tomb! When you follow Jesus closely, you, too, will see amazing things happen. But don't forget to tell others!

Job

Who is Job?

Rich man of the East

When did he live?

No one knows for sure. Maybe 4,000 years ago!

What's his story?

One word: Patient

In more words: Job was a very good man with lots of animals, land, and children. One day, God let Satan test Job. So Satan had all of Job's things and children taken away from him. He even gave Job boils on his skin. But Job kept trusting God.

Job also

- was married to a woman who told him to curse God and die;
- had a long conversation with God Himself!
- ended up with more at the end than he had at the beginning.

What's an important verse about him?

People who don't give up are blessed. You have heard that Job was patient. And you have seen what the Lord finally did for him. JAMES 5:11

So what?

No matter how good you may be, bad things can still happen. But be patient. Stick with God, and everything will turn out all right in the end!

Jochebed

Who is Jochebed?

Wife of Amram; mother of Moses, Aaron, and Miriam

When did she live?

About 3,500 years ago

What's her story?

One word: Clever

In more words: When Moses was born, the Egyptian king ordered that all the Hebrew boy babies be killed. So Jochebed saved her baby, Moses, by putting him in a basket and hiding him in the river. There the king's daughter saw him and raised him as her own.

What's an important verse about her?

"Take this baby and nurse him for me," the princess told the baby's mother. "I will pay you for your help." So the woman took her baby home and nursed him. EXODUS 2:9 NLT

So what?

When you use your brain and, more importantly, trust God, He will reward you!

John the Apostle

Who is John the Apostle?

Brother of James; son of Salome
and Zebedee; disciple of Jesus; writer

When did he live?

About 2,000 years ago

What's his story?

One word: Loved

In more words: John the Apostle wrote the book of
John in the Bible. There he calls himself "the disciple
Jesus loved." John also wrote 1 John, 2 John, 3 John, and
Revelation. While Jesus was on the cross, He told John to
take care of Mary, Jesus' mother. And he did.

What's an important verse about him?

Dear children, let's not merely say that we love each other;
let us show the truth by our actions.
1 JOHN 3:18 NLT

So what?

Jesus loves you very much. Will you, like John, show Jesus'
love to someone else today?

John the Baptist

Who is John the Baptist?

Son of Zechariah and Elizabeth; cousin of Jesus

When did he live?

About 2,000 years ago

What's his story?

One word: Pointer

In more words: The angel Gabriel told Zechariah that he and his wife would have a child in their old age. That child was John the Baptist. He wore weird clothes and ate locusts. But when he saw Jesus, he knew He was the Son of God. And John pointed everyone to Him!

John the Baptist also

- baptized lots of people;
- saw the Holy Spirit land on Jesus, like a dove;
- was beheaded by Herod Antipas.

What's an important verse about him?

[John said,] "I am filled with joy at [Jesus'] success. He must become greater and greater, and I must become less and less."

JOHN 3:29–30 NLT

So what?

To be a true follower of Jesus, we must make knowing Jesus more important than anything we do well or right. For what can you praise Jesus—instead of yourself—today?

Jonah

Who is Jonah?

Prophet

When did he live?

About 2,700 years ago

What's his story?

One word: Runaway

In more words: God told Jonah to go to Nineveh to talk to people there. But Jonah was afraid, so he jumped on a ship going the other way. After he was thrown overboard, a sea creature swallowed Jonah. After Jonah prayed to God, the creature spit him out on land, and Jonah went to Nineveh.

What's an important verse about him?

Now the LORD had arranged for a great fish to swallow Jonah. And Jonah was inside the fish for three days and three nights. JONAH 1:17 NLT

So what?

When God asks you to do something, it's better to obey than run away. What has God been asking you to do?

Jonathan

Who is Jonathan?

Son of King Saul

When did he live?

About 3,000 years ago

What's his story?

One word: Friend

In more words: Jonathan was a good leader of his father's army and also David's best friend. When King Saul wanted to kill David, Jonathan risked his own life and his dad's anger to save David. Later, Jonathan died on the battlefield as he fought for his father.

What's an important verse about him?

The soul of Jonathan became one with the soul of David. Jonathan loved him as himself.
1 SAMUEL 18:1 NLV

So what?

Look for a good friend who shares your faith in God. That will be a friendship you will always treasure, one that will gladden your heart.

Joseph of Arimathea

Who is Joseph of Arimathea?

Member of the Jewish Council

When did he live?

About 2,000 years ago

What's his story?

One word: Bold

In more words: When the Jewish leaders decided that Jesus should be put to death, Councilman Joseph of Arimathea did not agree. That's because he was a follower of Jesus. But he had kept this a secret because he feared what the Jews might do to him.

What's an important verse about him?

Joseph went boldly to Pilate and asked for Jesus' body. . . . He put it in a tomb cut out of rock. MARK 15:43, 46

So what?

At first you might be afraid of someone or something. But in the end, God will give you the courage to do what's right.

Joseph, Foster Father of Jesus

Who is Joseph

Carpenter; husband of Mary

When did he live?

About 2,000 years ago

What's his story?

One word: Guided

In more words: Four times an angel of the Lord talked to Joseph in a dream. First, an angel told him to marry the already-pregnant Mary. Second, to keep baby Jesus safe, the angel told Joseph to take Jesus to Egypt. Third, the angel told him to go back to Israel, and the fourth message was to head to Galilee.

What's an important verse about him?

Joseph awoke from his sleep. He did what the angel of the Lord told him to do. MATTHEW 1:24 NLV

So what?

Once you start to follow God's orders, He will continue to guide you—over and over again.

Joseph, Son of Jacob

Shepherd, slave, prisoner, ruler

When did he live?

About 4,000 years ago

What's his story?

One word: Dreamer

In more words: Joseph dreamed he would rule over his father and brothers someday. After he told his family about his dream, his brothers sold him to traveling salesmen. So Joseph went from shepherd to slave to prisoner—but ended up a ruler in Egypt.

Joseph also

- wore a really colorful coat;
- told people what their dreams meant;
- never lost hope in God.

What's an important verse about him?

"You planned to do a bad thing to me. But God planned it for good, to make it happen that many people should be kept alive, as they are today."

GENESIS 50:20 NLV

So what?

If things don't go as planned, don't give up or get upset. Just do the next thing! Keep hoping in God. He will turn whatever seems bad into something that will get you one step closer to your dreams!

Joshua

Who is Joshua?

Moses' assistant; Israel's next leader

When did he live?

About 3,400 years ago

What's his story?

One word: Loyal

In more words: When Moses sent men out to look over the Promised Land, only Caleb and Joshua said that the Israelites could defeat the giants in that land. Joshua led many battles, including the one at Jericho. When Moses died, Joshua became the Jews' next leader.

Joshua also

- led God's people into the Promised Land;
- always obeyed God;
- defeated 31 kings.

What's an important verse about him?

"Choose today whom you will serve. . . . As for me and my family, we will serve the LORD." JOSHUA 24:15 NLT

So what?

Joshua is a good example of what happens when we serve God—and God alone. When you stick to God, you can be sure He will stick to you!

Josiah

Who is Josiah?

Sixteenth king of Judah

When did he live?

About 2,600 years ago

What's his story?

One word: Focused

In more words: When he was eight, Josiah became king and had the temple fixed up. There, a book of Moses' Law was found. The good and great King Josiah had it read to him. Then he read it to his people.

What's an important verse about him?

There was no king like Josiah. . . . He followed the LORD with all his heart and all his soul. . .with all his strength. He did everything the Law of Moses required.
2 KINGS 23:25

So what?

When your eyes and heart are on God's Word, He will lead you—to be the best you can be!

Judas Iscariot

Who is Judas Iscariot?

Disciple of Jesus

When did he live?

About 2,000 years ago

What's his story?

One word: Traitor

In more words: Keeper of the disciples' money bag, Judas often stole coins for himself. He was later paid thirty silver pieces for leading temple guards to Gethsemane. There Judas kissed Jesus so the soldiers would know whom to arrest. Afterward, Judas felt bad for what he'd done.

What's an important verse about him?

"I have sinned," he said. "I handed over a man who is not guilty." . . . Judas threw the money into the temple and left. Then he went away and hanged himself.
MATTHEW 27:4–5

So what?

To truly follow Jesus, love God and others more than money and yourself!

Lazarus

Who is Lazarus?

Brother of Mary and Martha

When did he live?

About 2,000 years ago

What's his story?

One word: Glory

In more words: Lazarus, Jesus' friend, was sick. His sisters sent a message to Jesus. But Jesus stayed where He was. By the time Jesus got to His friend, Lazarus had been dead for four days. It didn't matter. Jesus raised him from the dead! And many then believed!

What's an important verse about him?

Jesus. . .said, "Lazarus's sickness will not end in death. No, it happened for the glory of God so that the Son of God will receive glory from this."
JOHN 11:4 NLT

So what?

Never moan. God can make something good come out of anything!

Leah

Who is Leah?

First wife of Jacob; sister of Rachel

When did she live?

About 4,000 years ago

What's her story?

One word: Unloved

In more words: One night Jacob was to marry the woman he loved—Rachel, Laban's younger daughter. But Laban sent Leah into the dark tent instead of Rachel, thus tricking Jacob into marrying the older sister. An ancestor of Jesus, Leah gave Jacob six sons.

What's an important verse about her?

The LORD saw that Jacob didn't love Leah as much as he loved Rachel. So he let Leah have children. But Rachel wasn't able to. GENESIS 29:31

So what?

Even if, like Leah, you feel unloved, just keep your faith in God. He will bless and love you all the more!

Lot

Who is Lot?

Abraham's nephew

When did he live?

About 4,000 years ago

What's his story?

One word: Drifter

In more words: Lot and Abraham had so many animals, there wasn't enough land for the men to stay together. So Lot chose to go live near the evil city of Sodom. The farther from Abraham he got, the further he drifted into trouble. But because Lot kept trusting God, angels rescued him.

What's an important verse about him?

God saved Lot. He was a man who did what was right. He was shocked by the dirty, sinful lives of people who didn't obey God's laws.

2 PETER 2:7

So what?

Even if trouble is all around you, don't be afraid. Trust God. He'll save you!

Luke

Who is Luke?

Doctor; missionary; writer; follower of Jesus

When did he live?

About 2,000 years ago

What's his story?

One word: Reporter

In more words: Luke wrote the Bible book called Luke. There he gives all the facts of Jesus' life and the miracles He did. Luke also wrote the Bible book of Acts, in which he tells of mission trips he had with the apostle Paul.

What's an important verse about him?

I have looked with care into these things from the beginning. I have decided it would be good to write them to you one after the other the way they happened. Then you can be sure you know the truth about the things you have been taught. LUKE 1:3–4 NLV

So what?

You, too, can be a fact-seeker. Take time each day to read God's truth in the Bible!

Lydia

Seller of cloth; first European Christian

When did she live?

About 2,000 years ago

What's her story?

One word: Open

In more words: Lydia was a woman who sold expensive purple cloth. Seeing her and other women sitting on a riverbank at a prayer meeting, Paul sat down and spoke to them. Lydia believed what Paul was saying. So she and her whole house were baptized!

What's an important verse about her?

As [Lydia] listened to us, the Lord opened her heart, and she accepted what Paul was saying. ACTS 16:14 NLT

So what?

Next time you hear or read God's Word, be like Lydia. Open up your ears—and your heart!

Mark

Who is Mark?

Gospel writer; also called John Mark

When did he live?

About 2,000 years ago

What's his story?

One word: Runner

In more words: When Jesus was arrested, one young man, probably Mark, ran away so fast he left his clothes behind! Mark also went on a mission trip with Paul and Barnabas, only to run off in the middle of it. Mark made some mistakes, but in the end, he helped Paul and others.

What's an important verse about him?

[The apostle Paul wrote:] Only Luke is with me. Get Mark and bring him with you. He helps me in my work for the Lord. 2 TIMOTHY 4:11

So what?

It's okay if you make mistakes—as long as you learn and grow from them.

Martha

Who is Martha?

Sister of Mary and Lazarus

When did she live?

About 2,000 years ago

What's her story?

One word: Busy

In more words: When Jesus was at Martha's house, her sister, Mary, sat at Jesus' feet, listening to Him. That made Martha. So Martha whined to Jesus. She wanted Him to tell Mary to help her make dinner!

What's an important verse about her?

"Martha, Martha," the Lord answered. "You are worried and upset about many things. But only one thing is needed. Mary has chosen what is better. And it will not be taken away from her." LUKE 10:41–42

So what?

You probably have lots to do. But spending time with Jesus is the best thing to do!

Mary Magdalene

Who is Mary Magdalene?

Follower of Jesus

When did she live?

About 2,000 years ago

What's her story?

One word: Free

In more words: Jesus chased seven demons out of Mary Magdalene. Because of that, she was a very thankful follower. She gave money to support Jesus and His disciples. Mary was one of the few with Jesus when He died on the cross. She was the first to see Him after His death.

Mary Magdalene also
- brought burial spices to anoint Jesus' body;
- saw the stone rolled away from Jesus' tomb;
- spoke to two angels.

What's an important verse about her?

Mary Magdalene found the disciples and told them, "I have seen the Lord!" Then she gave them his message. JOHN 20:18 NLT

So what?

Jesus has freed you from sin. Have you told anyone about Him today?

Mary of Bethany

Who is Mary of Bethany?

Sister of Martha and Lazarus

When did she live?

About 2,000 years ago

What's her story?

One word: Remembered

In more words: Mary of Bethany wanted to spend time being with and listening to Jesus. She did that rather than preparing dinner for her guests. She left that work to her sister, Martha. Her loyalty to Jesus will never be forgotten.

What's an important verse about her?

"She has poured this perfume on me to prepare my body for burial. I tell you the truth, wherever the Good News is preached throughout the world, this woman's deed will be remembered and discussed."
MATTHEW 26:12–13 NLT

So what?

Spend lots of time hanging with Jesus and you, too, will be remembered!

Mary, Mother of Jesus

Who is Mary, mother of Jesus?

Mother of God's Son; wife of Joseph

When did she live?

About 2,000 years ago

What's her story?

One word: Wonderer

In more words: The angel Gabriel came and told Mary she would be the mother of God's Son. And she was. After she gave birth to Jesus, angels spoke to shepherds, telling them where they could find Christ the Lord. When they visited Jesus and told their story, Mary wondered about their words.

Mary also

- was an ordinary woman yet an extraordinary servant of God;
- saw Jesus change water into wine;
- was with Jesus at His death.

What's an important verse about her?

Mary said, "I am willing to be used of the Lord. Let it happen to me as you have said." Then the angel went away from her. LUKE 1:38 NLV

So what?

Mary was willing to be used by God—mind, body, and spirit. Because of that, amazing things happened in her life. Are you a willing servant of God?

Matthew

Who is Matthew?

Follower of Jesus; writer; also called Levi

When did he live?

About 2,000 years ago

What's his story?

One word: Tracker

   In more words: Matthew collected and kept track of taxes. When he left everything to follow Jesus, God used Matthew's talents in a new way. Matthew kept track of Jesus' doings on earth and wrote them out for us—in the Bible book of Matthew!

What's an important verse about him?

He walked farther and saw Levi (Matthew). . .sitting at his work gathering taxes. Jesus said to him, "Follow Me." Levi got up and followed Him. MARK 2:14 NLV

So what?

Are you following Jesus? If so, how is God using you in a new way?

Melchizedek

Who is Melchizedek?

King of Salem; priest of God Most High

When did he live?

About 4,000 years ago

What's his story?

One word: Mysterious

In more words: Melchizedek met Abraham one day. He reminded Abraham to give God the praise for a victory in battle. Then Melchizedek disappeared from scripture. Some people think this Old Testament priest was actually Jesus.

What's an important verse about him?

Melchizedek has no father or mother. He has no family line. His days have no beginning. His life has no end. He remains a priest forever, just like the Son of God.
HEBREWS 7:3

So what?

When things go well, do you praise God? After all, it's no mystery that it's His doing, right?

Methuselah

Who is Methuselah?

Son of Enoch

When did he live?

Thousands of years ago

What's his story?

One word: Ancient

In more words: Methuselah is the oldest of the old! He is the longest-living human being recorded in the Bible. He was 187 years old when he became the father of Lamech. Although Methuselah's father, Enoch, went up with God, Methuselah did eventually pass away—but only after having other sons and daughters.

What's an important verse about him?

Methuselah lived 969 years, and he died.
GENESIS 5:27 NLV

So what?

God decides how long you will live. But only you can decide what you will do while you're here. Will you use your time to help God and love others?

Miriam

Who is Miriam?

Sister of Aaron and Moses

When did she live?

About 3,500 years ago

What's her story?

One word: Green-eyed

In more words: Miriam was a good sister to Moses—until she and Aaron tried to bring him down. Because of her green-eyed jealousy of Moses, God gave Miriam leprosy, a skin-eating disease. Moses, a good brother, asked God to heal his sister. And God did.

What's an important verse about her?

Miriam and Aaron spoke against Moses. . . . "Is it true that the Lord has spoken only through Moses? Has He not spoken through us also?" NUMBERS 12:1–2 NLV

So what?

Take care not to raise yourself up by bringing down someone you envy. That kind of jealousy will only eat away at you.

Mordecai

Who is Mordecai?

Relative of Esther

When did he live?

About 2,500 years ago

What's his story?

One word: Refuser

In more words: Haman, one of King Xerxes' officials, was mad. Whenever he walked by, Mordecai refused to bow. Mordecai would worship no one but God. So Haman made plans to have Mordecai and all other Jews killed. Later, it turned out Haman had to bow to Mordecai—and Haman was killed.

What's an important verse about him?

Mordecai the Jew. . .found favor in the eyes of his people. He worked for the good of his people and spoke for the well-being of all the Jews. ESTHER 10:3 NLV

So what?

When you worship only God—and not people— only good will come of it.

Moses

Who is Moses?

Son of Jochebed and Amram; brother of Aaron and Miriam; husband of Zipporah; writer of first five Old Testament books

About 3,500 years ago

One word: Self-doubting

In more words: Out of a burning bush, God spoke to Moses. God said He would be sending Moses to Pharaoh, asking him to let God's people out of Egypt. But Moses doubted he could do all God wanted. God disagreed. He had already prepared Moses to do the deeds—and Moses did.

Moses also
- was raised by Pharaoh's daughter;
- killed an Egyptian who was beating a Jewish slave;
- ran away and became a shepherd;
- parted the Red Sea;
- received God's Law on two stone tablets;
- led the Israelites to the Promised Land.

Moses protested to God, "Who am I to appear before Pharaoh? Who am I to lead the people of Israel out of Egypt?" God answered, "I will be with you."
EXODUS 3:11–12 NLT

Since then, Israel has never had a prophet like Moses. The LORD knew him face to face. Moses did many miraculous signs and wonders. The LORD had sent him to do them in Egypt. DEUTERONOMY 34:10–11

So what?

No matter who you are, you can do what God calls you to do—because He is with you!

If you trust God, He will give you the power to do amazing things! Seek His face today and find out what He wants you to do.

Naaman

Who is Naaman?

Army commander

When did he live?

About 2,900 years ago

What's his story?

One word: Prideful

In more words: Naaman was an army hero with leprosy, a skin disease. His wife's servant girl told him a prophet of Israel, Elisha, could heal him. When Naaman went to see the prophet, Elisha didn't come out but sent a message to wash in the Jordan seven times. That hurt Naaman's pride.

What's an important verse about him?

Naaman went away angry. He said, "I was sure he would come out to me."
2 Kings 5:11

So what?

Once Naaman swallowed his pride, he went down to the river, washed, and was healed. He teaches you to not let pride stand in the way of God's work in your life.

Naomi

Who is Naomi?

Wife of Elimelech; mother-in-law of Ruth

When did she live?

About 3,200 years ago

What's her story?

One word: Hopeful

In more words: Naomi and her family moved from Israel to Moab during a drought. There, Naomi's husband and sons died. She was very sad. So she decided to go back to Israel. Ruth, her daughter-in-law, went with her. There, Naomi became a grandmother.

What's an important verse about her?

Naomi said to her daughter-in-law. . . ."The LORD is still being kind to those who are living and those who are dead." RUTH 2:20

So what?

No matter how bad things look, keep hoping. God will not fail you.

Nathan

Who is Nathan?

Prophet

When did he live?

About 3,000 years ago

What's his story?

One word: Adviser

In more words: King David wanted to build a temple for the Lord. But God told Nathan to tell David that Solomon was to build God's house. David was very disappointed. Then God, speaking through Nathan, told David that the Lord had other plans—like David's son (Jesus) taking over another kind of throne.

What's an important verse about him?

"I will never take my love away from your son. I will place him over my house and my kingdom forever. His throne will last forever." 1 CHRONICLES 17:13–14

So what?

God puts wise people in our lives to help us. Who can you ask for advice?

Nebuchadnezzar

Who is Nebuchadnezzar?

King of Babylon

When did he live?

About 2,600 years ago

What's his story?

One word: Braggart

In more words: One day while walking on his palace roof, King Nebuchadnezzar bragged about his great deeds, power, and palace. That's when God told Nebuchadnezzar he would change into a beast. Later, when Nebuchadnezzar came to his senses, he became a king again.

What's an important verse about him?

My body became wet with the dew of heaven. I stayed that way until my hair grew like the feathers of an eagle. My nails became like the claws of a bird. DANIEL 4:33

So what?

Beastly pride can turn you into an animal. Stay humble and human by thanking God for all you've got.

Nehemiah

Who is Nehemiah?

Prophet; king's wine taster

When did he live?

About 2,500 years ago

What's his story?

One word: Builder

In more words: Nehemiah heard about Jerusalem's broken-down wall. Its gates had been burned. This made him sad. The king told Nehemiah he could leave Iran and go fix Jerusalem's wall. Because of his great faith in God, Nehemiah and the people rebuilt the wall in only fifty-two days!

What's an important verse about him?

"The God of heaven will help us succeed. We, his servants, will start rebuilding this wall." NEHEMIAH 2:20 NLT

So what?

Put all your trust in God and put your hand to the task He gives you. Then He will make what seems undoable doable!

Nicodemus

Who is Nicodemus?

Jewish council member and Pharisee

When did he live?

About 2,000 years ago

What's his story?

One word: Learner

In more words: Nicodemus was a well-thought-of Jewish teacher. He went to talk to Jesus at night, when others wouldn't see him. Nicodemus asked Jesus several questions, which Jesus answered. After dying on the cross, Jesus was buried by Joseph of Arimathea and Nicodemus.

What's an important verse about him?

Jesus replied, "You are a respected Jewish teacher, and yet you don't understand these things?" JOHN 3:10 NLT

So what?

If you have a question, go to Jesus and His Word. People willing to learn are always growing closer to God—in heaven and on earth.

Noah

Who is Noah?

Ark builder

When did he live?

Thousands of years ago

What's his story?

One word: Boatman

In more words: People on earth were behaving badly. So God decided to start over with good Noah and his family. God told him to build an ark and fill it with animals, two by two. Then Noah's family got on the boat to be safe from the flood that came with forty days and nights of rain.

Noah also

- built the ark in 120 years;
- had three sons;
- lived 950 years.

What's an important verse about him?

God. . .brought the flood on the world of sinners. But Noah was a preacher of right living. He and his family of seven were the only ones God saved.
2 PETER 2:5 NLV

So what?

If you do right by God, He will do right by you.

Paul

Who is Paul?

Pharisee known as Saul; killer of Christians; preacher to Christians; tentmaker and writer

When did he live?

About 2,000 years ago

What's his story?

One word: Missionary

In more words: Saul mistreated many Christians. Then, while he was on the road, he saw a flash of light and fell to the ground. He heard Jesus speak from heaven, asking why Saul was against Him. When Saul's friends led him away, he was blind. Later, Saul was healed and believed in Jesus Christ. Once Saul, now Paul, he traveled the world, spreading the Good News.

Paul also

- gave the okay to stone Stephen;
- took three missionary journeys;
- spent lots of time in prisons;
- wrote many letters to churches;
- was shipwrecked on the island of Malta;
- lived after getting bitten by a poisonous snake.

What's an important verse about him?

I focus on this one thing: Forgetting the past and looking forward to what lies ahead, I press on to reach the end of the race and receive the heavenly prize for which God, through Christ Jesus, is calling us. PHILIPPIANS 3:13–14 NLT

So what?

Don't worry about what happened yesterday. Focus on winning with Jesus today!

Peter

Who is Peter?

Fisherman; brother of Andrew; disciple of Jesus; also called Simon Peter

When did he live?

About 2,000 years ago

What's his story?

One word: Rock

In more words: Peter was one of three disciples closest to Jesus. But Jesus told Peter that three times he would deny knowing Jesus, and then a rooster would crow. And that's just what happened after Jesus was arrested. Three times a frightened Peter told people that he didn't know Jesus. Then Peter heard "Cock-a-doodle-doo!"

Peter also

- healed many people;
- spent time in prison;
- wrote the Bible books of 1 and 2 Peter.

What's an important verse about him?

"And I tell you that you are Peter. On this rock I will build My church. The powers of hell will not be able to have power over My church." MATTHEW 16:18 NLV

So what?

Jesus can use you for great things—even if you make mistakes.

Philemon

Who is Philemon?

Friend of Paul; "owner" of Onesimus

When did he live?

About 2,000 years ago

What's his story?

One word: Master

In more words: Onesimus, Philemon's slave, had run away from Philemon and met up with Paul in prison. Onesimus became a Christian. In his letter, Paul tells Philemon he is sending Onesimus back and hopes Philemon will treat the man as a brother, not as a slave.

What's an important verse about him?

Any favor you do must be done because you want to do it, not because you have to. PHILEMON 1:14

So what?

God loves people who truly want to help brothers and sisters. What are you willing to do for others—and God—today?

Pontius Pilate

Who is Pontius Pilate?

Roman governor of Judea

When did he live?

About 2,000 years ago

What's his story?

One word: Appeaser

In more words: Pilate was an appeaser. That means he often gave in to what others wanted, even though he knew he was right! Pilate knew Jesus had committed no crime. But because the crowd demanded Jesus' death, Pilate caved.

What's an important verse about him?

Pilate wanted to satisfy the crowd. So he. . .ordered that Jesus be whipped. Then he handed him over to be nailed to a cross. MARK 15:15

So what?

Ask God for help when you are making decisions. He'll help you to do the right thing—even if it doesn't please someone else.

Priscilla

Who is Priscilla?

Wife of Aquila; tentmaker

When did she live?

About 2,000 years ago

What's her story?

One word: Coworker

In more words: Priscilla was a busy woman. She was not only a housewife and tentmaker, but she also traveled and worked with Paul, studied the Good News about Jesus, taught many people about Christ, held church services at her house—and more!

What's an important verse about her?

Priscilla and Aquila. . .almost died for me. I am thankful for them. All the churches that were started among the people who are not Jews are thankful for them also. ROMANS 16:3–4 NLV

So what?

When you work for Christ, there's no telling how much you will change the world for the good!

Rachel

Who is Rachel?

Wife of Jacob; mother of Joseph and Benjamin

When did she live?

About 4,000 years ago

What's her story?

One word: Dissatisfied

In more words: Rachel was very beautiful. Jacob truly loved her, not her sister, Leah. But neither of those things made Rachel happy. She demanded children from Jacob. But then, when she gave birth to her son Joseph, instead of being satisfied with one, she said, "May the Lord give me another son."

What's an important verse about her?

When Rachel saw that she had not given birth to any children for Jacob, she became jealous of her sister. She said to Jacob, "Give me children, or else I am going to die!" GENESIS 30:1 NLV

So what?

If you are satisfied and thankful for all that God has given you, He will give you more.

Rahab

Who is Rahab?

Body seller; ancestor of David and Jesus

When did she live?

About 3,400 years ago

What's her story?

One word: Spared

In more words: Rahab was a woman who sold to men the use of her body. When Joshua sent spies to check out Jericho, Rahab saved (or spared) them from being killed. That's because she had heard what their God had done and believed in His power.

What's an important verse about her?

Rahab, the prostitute, had faith. So she welcomed the spies. That's why she wasn't killed with those who didn't obey God. HEBREWS 11:31

So what?

God can use anyone. All you have to do is have faith and courage. Then He will do great things through you!

Rebekah

Who is Rebekah?

Isaac's wife; Esau and Jacob's mom

When did she live?

About 4,100 years ago

What's her story?

One word: Willful

In more words: Rebekah had twin boys—Esau and Jacob. She liked Jacob the best. But her husband, Isaac, liked Esau. When it was time for the older son, Esau, to get his father's blessing, Rebekah came up with a plan for Jacob to get the blessing instead. This made for problems later.

What's an important verse about her?

Esau hated Jacob because their father had given Jacob the blessing. And Esau began to scheme: "I will soon be mourning my father's death. Then I will kill my brother, Jacob." GENESIS 27:41 NLT

So what?

Things work out better when you follow God's will rather than your own.

Rhoda

Who is Rhoda?

Servant girl

When did she live?

About 2,000 years ago

What's her story?

One word: Overjoyed!

In more words: Rhoda worked at the house of Mary, the mother of John Mark. Many Christians were there one night. They were praying Peter would be freed from prison. And he was! An angel got him out. Afterward Peter went right to Mary's house and knocked on the door.

What's an important verse about her?

Rhoda came to open it. When she recognized Peter's voice, she was so overjoyed that, instead of opening the door, she ran back inside and told everyone, "Peter is standing at the door!" ACTS 12:13–14 NLT

So what?

When God answers your prayers, let everyone see your joy!

Ruth

Who is Ruth?

Moabite daughter-in-law of Naomi; widow of
Mahlon; wife of Boaz; mother of Obed

When did she live?

About 3,200 years ago

What's her story?

One word: Loyal

In more words: Naomi's husband and two married
sons died, leaving her all alone. So Naomi left Moab to
go back to Israel. Ruth, now a widow herself, went along,
not wanting to leave her mother-in-law. In Israel, Ruth
worked in Boaz's fields. Then he married her.

What's an important verse about her?

"I will go where you go. I will live where you live. Your
people will be my people. And your God will be my God."
RUTH 1:16–17 NLV

So what?

God loves it when His people are loyal to each other—
and Him.

Samson

Who is Samson?

Judge of Israel; son of Manoah

When did he live?

About 3,300 years ago

What's his story?

One word: Strongman

In more words: Samson was born to an old couple who had been visited by an angel. He was to be a Nazirite—set apart for God's use. But he broke the Nazirite rules. When Delilah cut his hair, Samson lost his strength. The Philistines gouged his eyes out and put him in prison.

Samson also

- killed a lion with his bare hands;
- killed 1,000 Philistines with the jawbone of a donkey;
- killed more Philistines at his death than he did in life.

What's an important verse about him?

Samson called to the Lord and said, "O Lord God, I beg You. Remember me. Give me strength only this once, O God. So I may now punish the Philistines for my two eyes." JUDGES 16:28 NLV

So what?

Even if you make mistakes, God can still use you—from the beginning of your life to the end.

Samuel

Who is Samuel?

Judge, prophet, priest of Israel; son of Elkanah and Hannah

When did he live?

About 4,100 years ago

What's his story?

One word: Listener

In more words: Samuel (which means "heard of God") was born in answer to his mother, Hannah's, prayer for a son. As a boy, he served Eli the priest. Later, Samuel put oil on the heads of Israel's first two kings, announcing them as picked by God.

What's an important verse about him?

Then the Lord came and stood and called as He did the other times, "Samuel! Samuel!" And Samuel said, "Speak, for Your servant is listening." 1 SAMUEL 3:10 NLV

So what?

Tell God you're listening. Then wait for Him to speak.

Sapphira

Who is Sapphira?

Ananias's wife

When did she live?

About 2,000 years ago

What's her story?

One word: Liar

In more words: Some Christians were selling their land and possessions, then giving the money to the church. Ananias and Sapphira sold some land—but Peter knew Ananias kept part of the money for himself. When he brought money to Peter, Ananias dropped dead.

What's an important verse about her?

Peter said to her, "How could you two have talked together about lying to the Holy Spirit? See! Those who buried your husband are standing at the door and they will carry you out also." At once she fell down at his feet and died.
ACTS 5:9–10 NLV

So what?

You can't hide anything from God. So be honest about everything to everyone—including Him.

Sarah

Who is Sarah?

Wife of Abraham; mother of Isaac

When did she live?

About 4,000 years ago

What's her story?

One word: Laughter

In more words: One day God visited Abraham. He told him that Abraham's wife, Sarah, would give birth to a son in one year. By then, Abraham would be 100 years old and Sarah would be 90. So she started laughing because she couldn't believe what God was promising! But you know what? Their son, Isaac, was born one year later!

What's an important verse about her?

"Is anything too hard for the Lord?"
GENESIS 18:14 NLV

So what?

Don't laugh off what seems undoable. Your God can do anything! That's what makes Him God!

Saul, King of Israel

Who is Saul, king of Israel?

First king God chose to rule Israel

When did he live?

About 3,000 years ago

What's his story?

One word: Rebel

In more words: Saul appeared to be handsome, brave, and obedient. But he made some pretty bad choices. Several times he disobeyed God. So God decided to replace Saul with David—someone who really loved and obeyed God from the heart.

What's an important verse about him?

"You haven't obeyed the command the LORD your God gave you. . . . Now your kingdom won't last."
1 SAMUEL 13:13–14

So what?

God wants you to obey Him—with all your mind and your heart and your soul.

Shiphrah

Who is Shiphrah?

Jewish midwife

When did she live?

About 3,500 years ago

What's her story?

One word: Daring

In more words: Shiphrah and Puah were Hebrews who helped other women give birth in Egypt. The king of Egypt told them to kill all the Jewish boy babies because there were so many Hebrews. Because Shiphrah and Puah loved God, they dared to disobey the king. They let the Hebrew baby boys live.

What's an important verse about her?

So God was good to the midwives, and the Israelites continued to multiply, growing more and more powerful. And because the midwives feared God, he gave them families of their own. EXODUS 1:20–21 NLT

So what?

God will reward you for your courage and obedience to Him.

Solomon

Who is Solomon?

King of Israel; son of David and Bathsheba; writer of Song of Solomon, Ecclesiastes, and many psalms and proverbs

When did he live?

About 3,000 years ago

What's his story?

One word: Wise

In more words: When Solomon became king, he didn't ask God for a long life, riches, or fame. Instead, Solomon asked for wisdom to rule. God was so pleased He gave the king not only wisdom but riches and honor as well. But when Solomon stopped looking to God for answers, trouble began.

Solomon also
- built God's temple;
- built his own palace;
- had a throne of ivory.

What's an important verse about him?

Trust in the LORD with all your heart;
  do not depend on your own understanding.
Seek his will in all you do,
  and he will show you which path to take.
PROVERBS 3:5–6 NLT

So what?

Need wisdom? Don't rely on your smarts. Go to God and His Word. He has lots of wisdom to share!

Stephen

Who is Stephen?

Faithful Christian; martyr

When did he live?

About 2,000 years ago

What's his story?

One word: Christlike

In more words: Stephen had lots of faith. He also was full of the Holy Spirit. He performed lots of miracles and preached to Jewish leaders. They got so mad that they dragged him out of the city and threw stones at him. Saul (later Paul) was a witness to this.

What's an important verse about him?

As they stoned him, Stephen prayed, "Lord Jesus, receive my spirit." He fell to his knees, shouting, "Lord, don't charge them with this sin!" And with that, he died. ACTS 7:59–60 NLT

So what?

To be like Christ, we must love all others—no matter what they do.

Thomas

Who is Thomas?

Disciple of Jesus; nicknamed the Twin

When did he live?

About 2,000 years ago

What's his story?

One word: Doubter

In more words: When Jesus rose from the grave, He appeared to all the disciples—except Thomas. When Thomas's other friends told him they'd seen the Lord, Thomas doubted them! One week later, Jesus appeared again to the disciples. Thomas was there—then he believed!

What's an important verse about him?

Jesus told him, "You believe because you have seen me. Blessed are those who believe without seeing me."
JOHN 20:29 NLT

So what?

Even though you haven't seen Jesus, you believe in Him. You are blessed because you have taken His Word as proof that He is real!

Timothy

Who is Timothy?

Missionary; pastor; friend of Paul the apostle

When did he live?

About 2,000 years ago

What's his story?

One word: Timid

In more words: Timothy was half Greek and half Jewish. When he met Paul, he became a Christian. He traveled with Paul on missionary journeys. Then he became a pastor at the church in Ephesus. Paul, who loved Timothy like a son, wrote him two letters, which are in the Bible.

What's an important verse about him?

God did not give us a spirit of fear. He gave us a spirit of power and of love and of a good mind. 2 TIMOTHY 1:7 NLV

So what?

Even if you are young and timid, God can give you the power to do great things. Soon you'll be bigger and bolder!

Titus

Who is Titus?

Greek man who became a Christian

When did he live?

About 2,000 years ago

What's his story?

One word: Helper

In more words: Titus traveled with Paul. Then Paul left him in charge of some churches. Titus was a very good preacher. When he was working at the church in Crete, Paul sent him a letter, giving him advice. The letter is called "Titus" and is a book in the Bible.

What's an important verse about him?

[Paul wrote:] Titus is my helper. He and I work together among you.
2 CORINTHIANS 8:23

So what?

God, His churches, and His leaders can use many helpers. What can you do to help God and your church today?

Zacchaeus

Who is Zacchaeus?
Tax collector

When did he live?
About 2,000 years ago

What's his story?
One word: Cheater

In more words: Zacchaeus was a greedy tax collector who cheated people. When he heard Jesus was coming to town, he wanted to see Him—but he was too short. So he climbed a tree. When Jesus saw Zacchaeus, He knew who he was right away.

What's an important verse about him?
Zacchaeus stood before the Lord and said, "I will give half my wealth to the poor, Lord, and if I have cheated people on their taxes, I will give them back four times as much!" LUKE 19:8 NLT

So what?
Jesus knows exactly who you are and what you've done. He knows that once you glimpse Him, you'll want to change.

Zechariah, Father of John the Baptist

Who is Zechariah, father of John the Baptist?

Husband of Elizabeth; priest at the temple

When did he live?

About 2,000 years ago

What's his story?

One word: Speechless

In more words: Zechariah was serving in the temple when the angel Gabriel came. He told Zechariah he would have a son named John. Old Zechariah didn't believe the angel. So Gabriel made it so Zechariah wouldn't be able to talk until the baby boy was born.

What's an important verse about him?

He wrote, "His name is John." Everyone was amazed. Right away Zechariah could speak again. His first words gave praise to God. LUKE 1:63–64

So what?

God can do awesome things through you, things so amazing they leave you speechless—except for praise!

Zipporah

Who is Zipporah?

Wife of Moses; daughter of Jethro

When did she live?

About 3,500 years ago

What's her story?

One word: Fixer

In more words: After murdering an Egyptian, Moses ran away to Midian. There he met Zipporah. The Lord was angry because Moses hadn't performed a Jewish ceremony on his son. So Zipporah did it—to save both Moses and their son.

What's an important verse about her?

She touched Moses' feet with the skin she had cut off. "You are a husband who has forced me to spill my son's blood," she said. So the Lord didn't kill Moses.
Exodus 4:25–26

So what?

It's never too late to fix your mistakes. God is always ready to forgive everything from A to Z.